21 GREAT CLASSICS

CONTENTS

JOHANN SEBASTIAN BACH	3	Air on the G String
	6	Jesu, Joy of Man's Desiring
LUDWIG VAN BEETHOVEN	9	Adagio cantabile (from Piano Sonata No. 8, "Pathétique")
ALEXANDER BORODIN	12	Polovetzian Dance (from *Prince Igor*)
JOHANNES BRAHMS	16	Hungarian Dance No. 5
	19	Waltz
ANTONÍN DVORÁK	22	Largo from Symphony No. 9 ("From the New World")(Excerpt)
GABRIEL FAURÉ	30	Sicilienne
CHARLES GOUNOD	34	Ave Maria
	37	Funeral March of a Marionette
EDVARD GRIEG	40	In the Hall of the Mountain King (from *Peer Gynt*)
GEORGE FRIDERIC HANDEL	27	Hallelujah! (from *Messiah*)
WOLFGANG AMADEUS MOZART	44	Eine kleine Nachtmusik (Excerpt)
	46	Symphony No. 40 in G Minor (Excerpt)
JACQUES OFFENBACH	51	Can Can (from *Orpheus in the Underworld*)
JOHANN PACHELBEL	54	Canon in D Major
JOHANN STRAUSS, JR.	58	Emperor Waltz
PYOTR IL'YICH TCHAIKOVSKY	62	Romeo and Juliet, "Love Theme"
	65	Swan Lake, Principal Theme
	68	Waltz of the Flowers (from *The Nutcracker*)
GIUSEPPE VERDI	60	La donna è mobile (from *Rigoletto*)

ISBN 978-0-634-02646-1

HAL•LEONARD®
CORPORATION
7777 W. BLUEMOUND RD. P.O. BOX 13819 MILWAUKEE, WI 53213

Visit Hal Leonard Online at
www.halleonard.com

PREFACE

It was a pivotal evening in my young life. A concert pianist had come to our small town and I was thrilled. The sounds he coaxed from the grand piano were unbelievable to me. I cannot recall everything he played that night, but Beethoven's "Pathétique" Sonata made a big impression. The passionate "Adagio" theme was one of the most beautiful things I had ever heard. I wanted to play it. Now! Fortunately for me, my very wise piano teacher did not say something like "well, Phillip, it will be *years* before you're ready for that piece." Instead, she found an arrangement that was playable for me (thank you, Mrs. Sherve!). This, and other classic themes, inspired a young boy with limited patience to keep studying the piano. I did learn the "real thing" eventually, but my memories of playing that simplified version of Ludwig's masterpiece are vivid and priceless.

Most of the themes in this collection were originally composed for ensemble situations including symphonic orchestra and opera. Others were originally written for the accomplished pianist. All of the arrangements have been carefully edited to maintain the spirit of the original work, while making the theme playable for the early level pianist.

If you have the chance to hear a recording or live performance of any of these pieces in their original form, your own interpretation at the piano will be much improved.

With best wishes,
Phillip Keveren

BIOGRAPHY

Phillip Keveren, a multi-talented keyboard artist and composer, has composed original works in a variety of genres from piano solo to symphonic orchestra. Mr. Keveren gives frequent concerts and workshops for teachers and their students in the United States, Canada, Europe, and Asia. Mr. Keveren holds a B.M. in composition from California State University Northridge and a M.M. in composition from the University of Southern California.

AIR ON THE G STRING

Johann Sebastian Bach
arranged by Phillip Keveren

Adagio

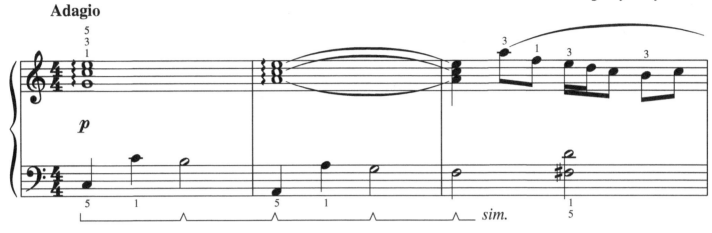

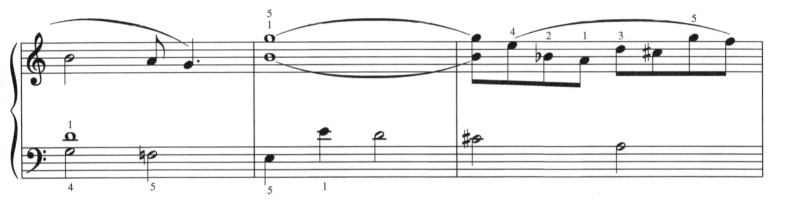

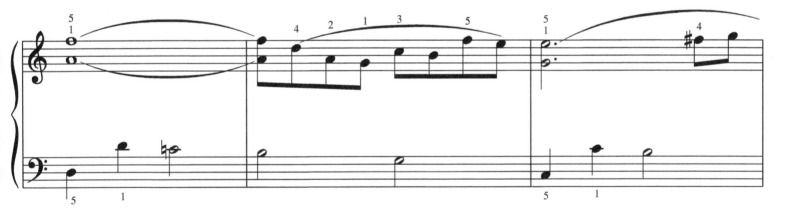

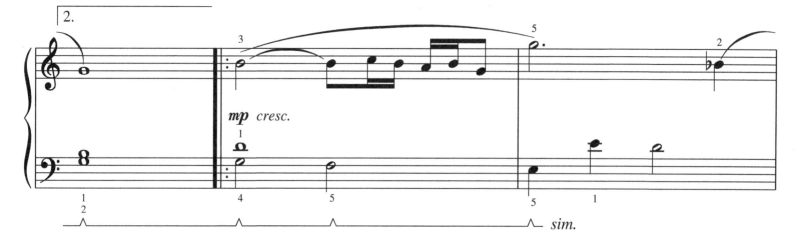

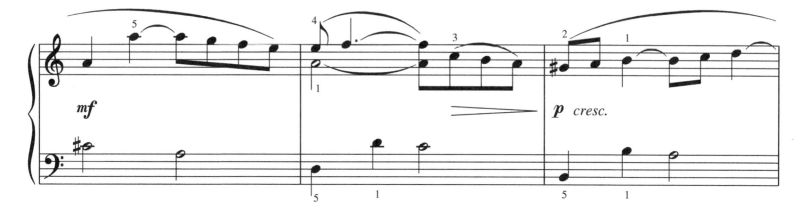

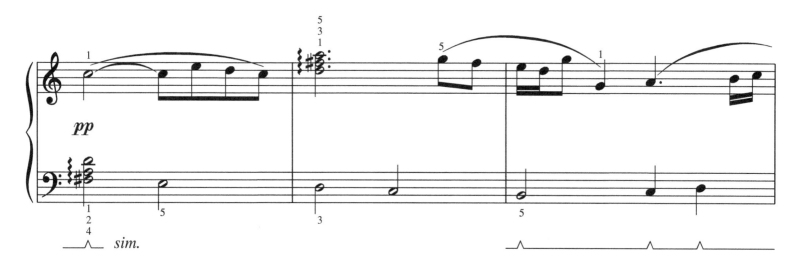

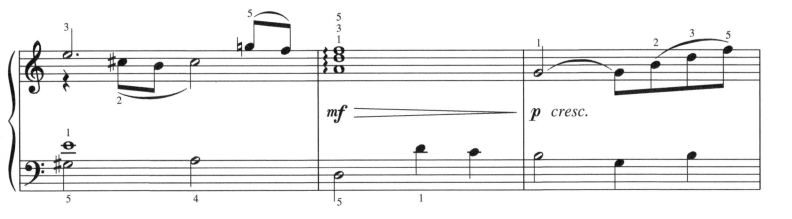

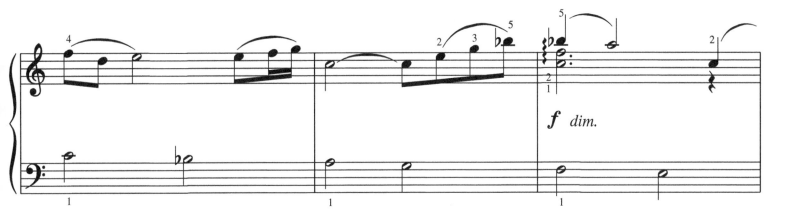

JESU, JOY OF MAN'S DESIRING

Johann Sebastian Bach
arranged by Phillip Keveren

Flowing gracefully

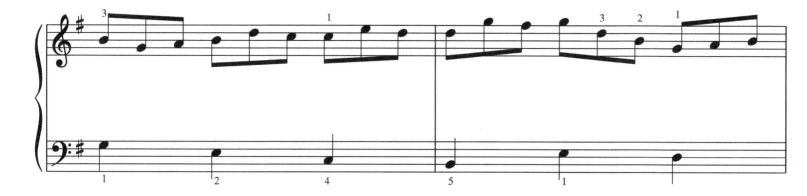

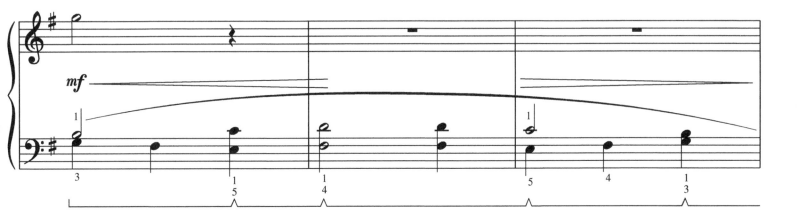

ADAGIO CANTABILE
Second Movement from Piano Sonata No. 8 ("Pathétique")

Ludwig van Beethoven
arranged by Phillip Keveren

Adagio cantabile

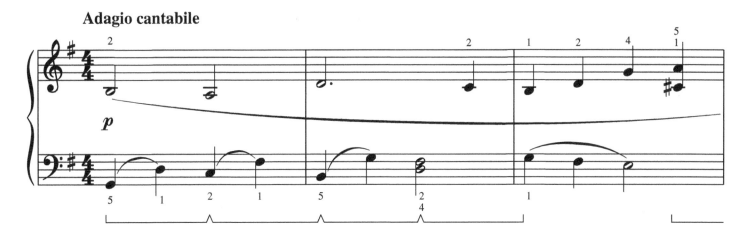

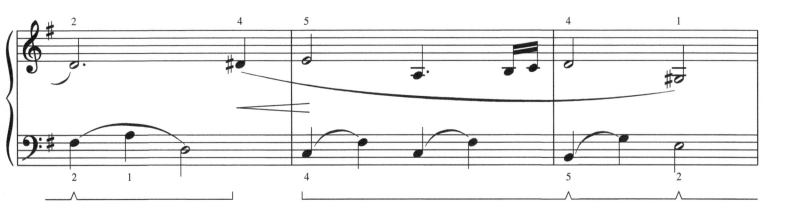

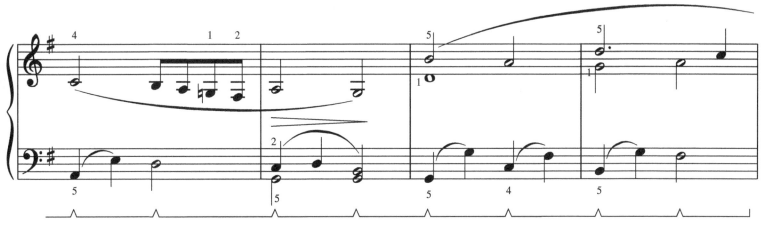

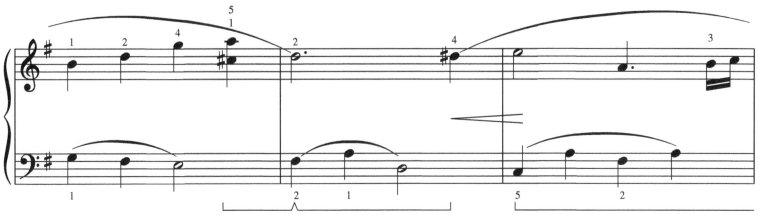

To Coda ⊕

D.C. al Coda

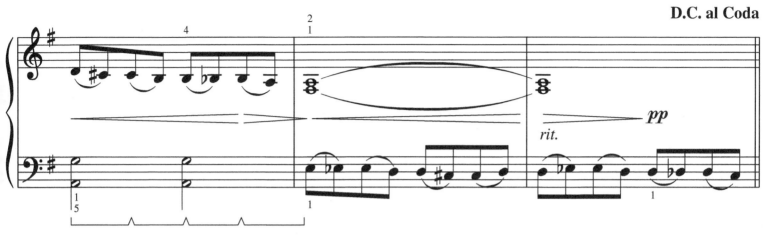

CODA

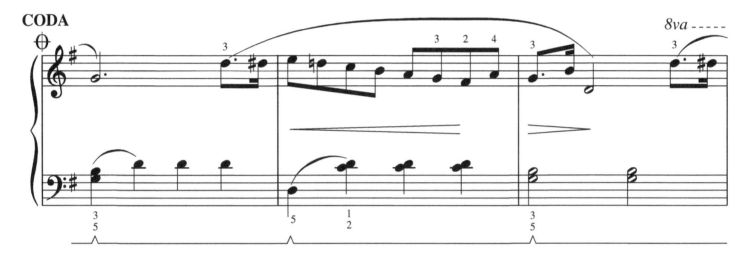

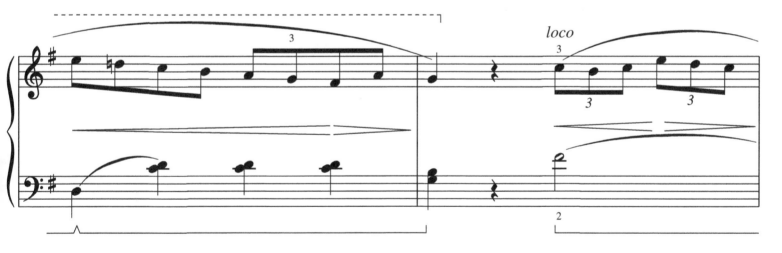

POLOVETZIAN DANCE

from *Prince Igor*

Alexander Borodin
arranged by Phillip Keveren

Andantino

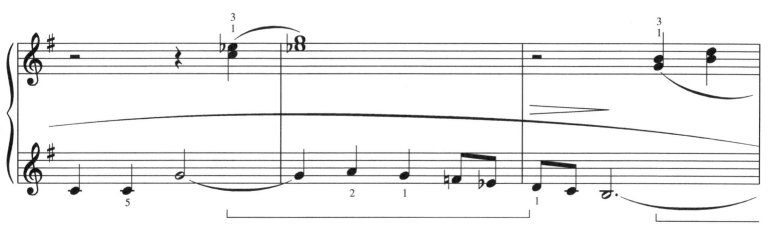

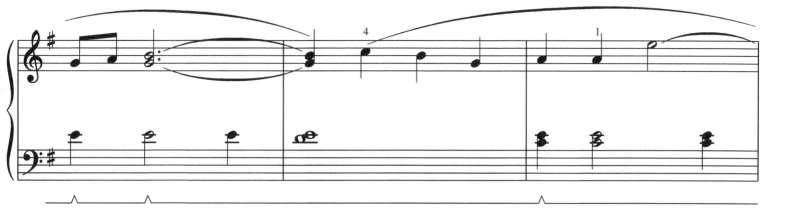

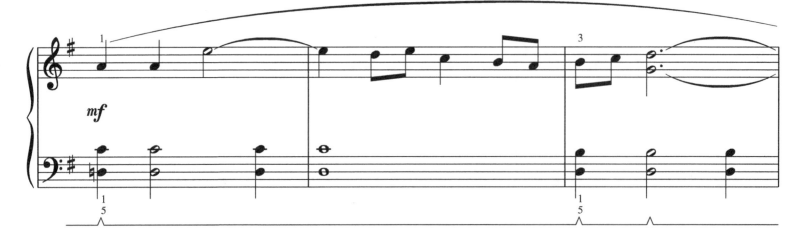

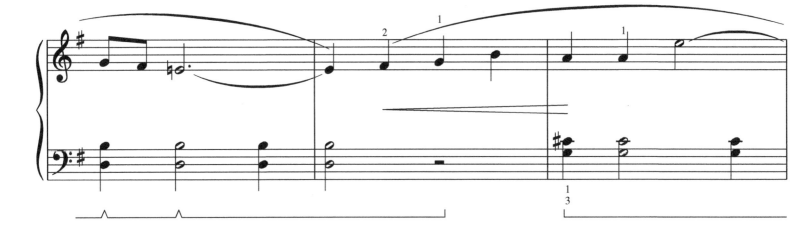

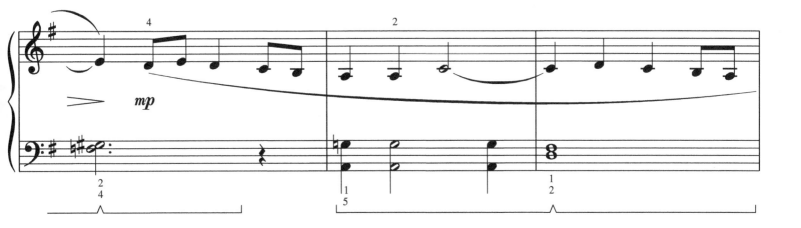

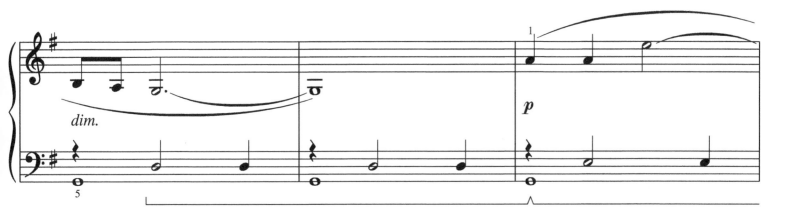

HUNGARIAN DANCE NO. 5

Johannes Brahms
arranged by Phillip Keveren

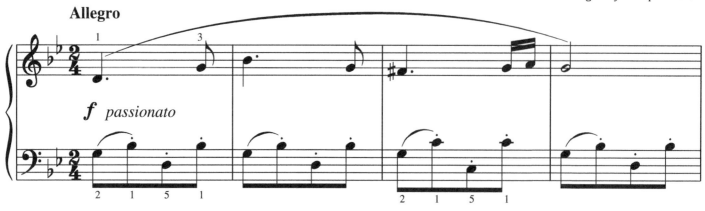

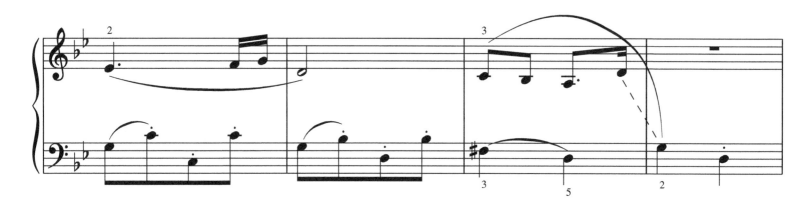

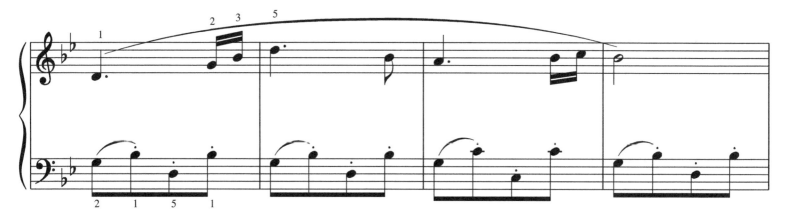

(no repeat on D.C.)

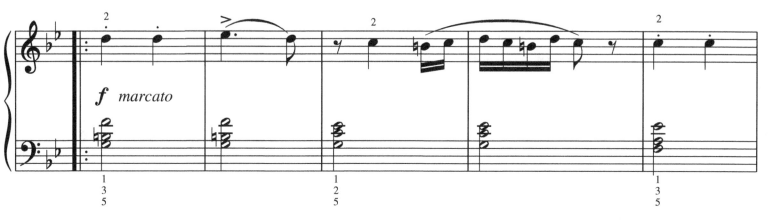

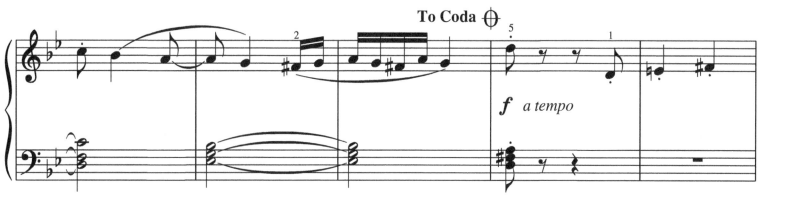

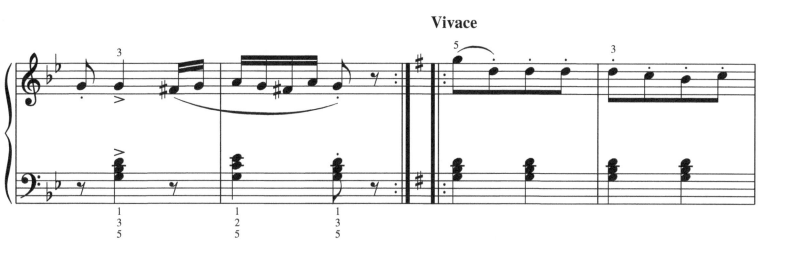

18

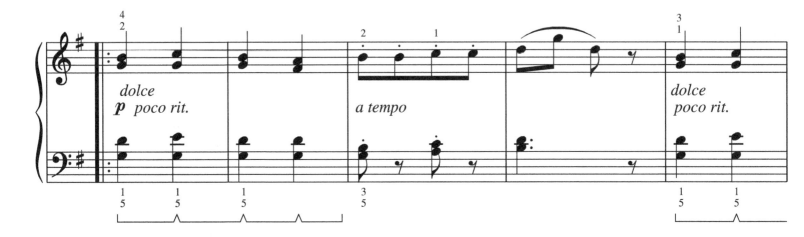

D.C. al Coda

CODA

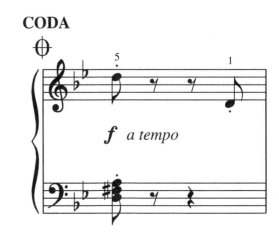

WALTZ, OP. 39, NO. 15

Johannes Brahms
arranged by Phillip Keveren

Gracefully

20

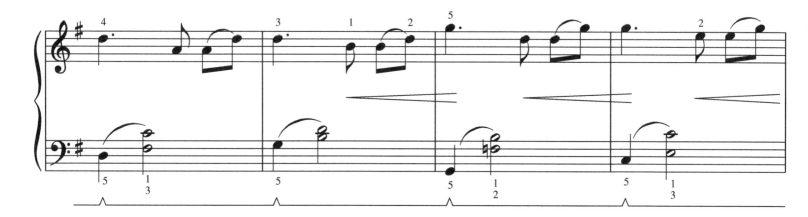

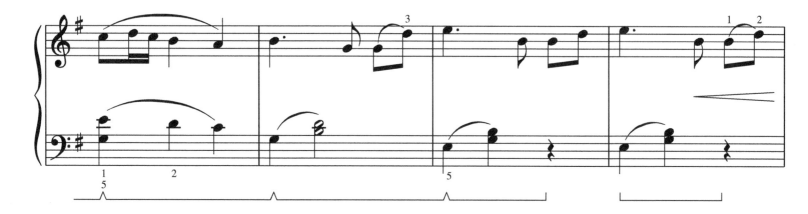

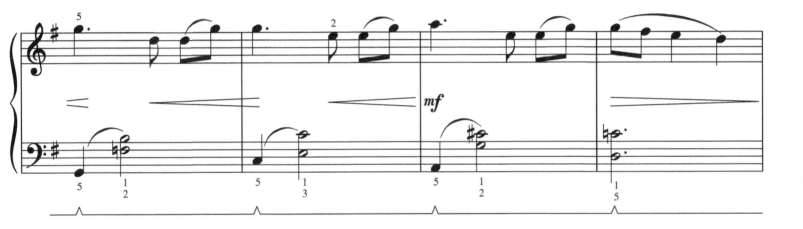

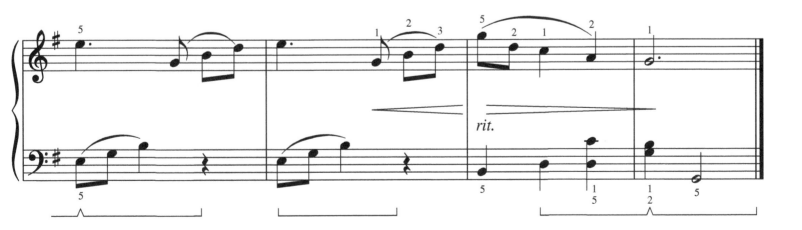

LARGO
from Symphony No. 9 ("From the New World")
Second Movement Excerpt

Antonín Dvořák
arranged by Phillip Keveren

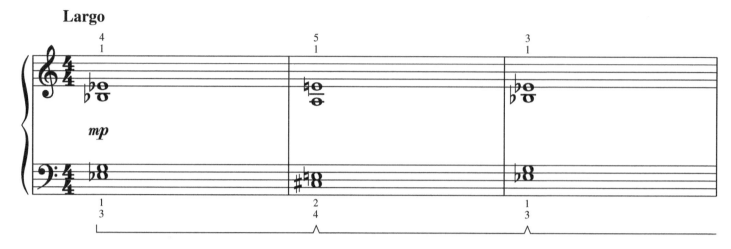

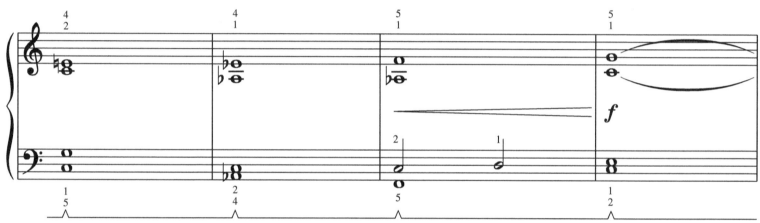

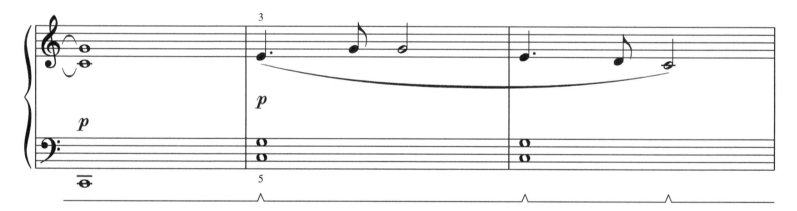

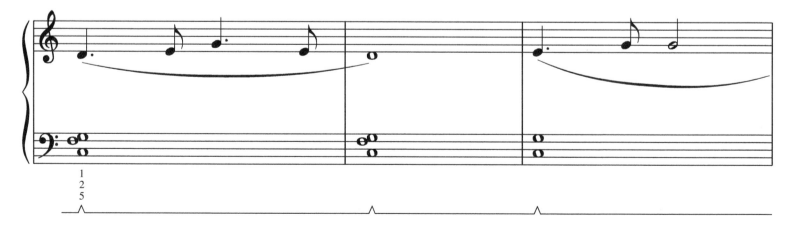

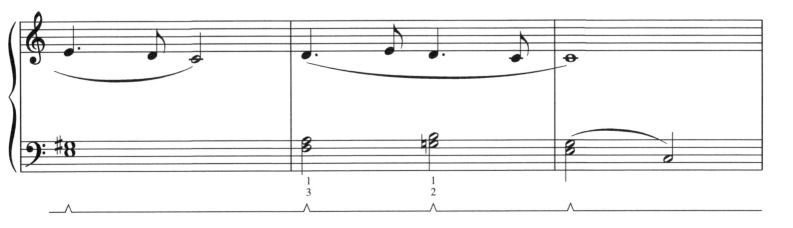

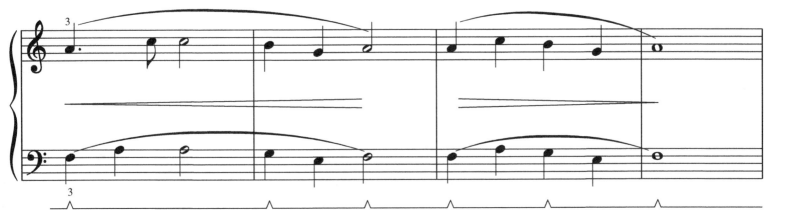

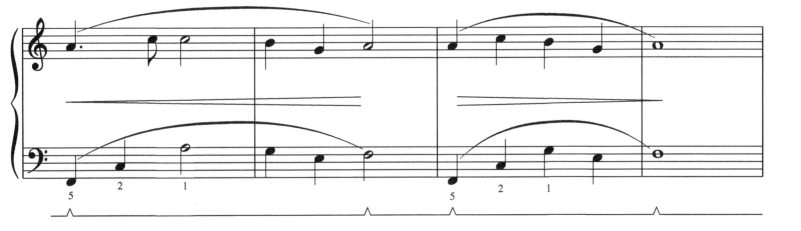

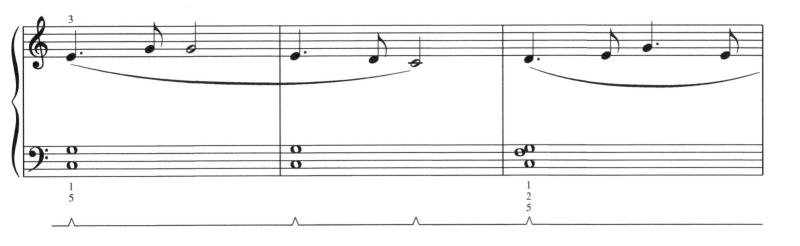

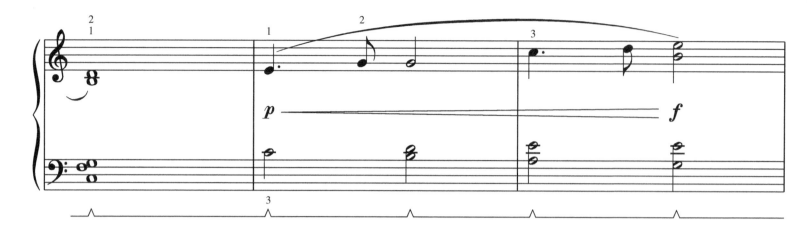

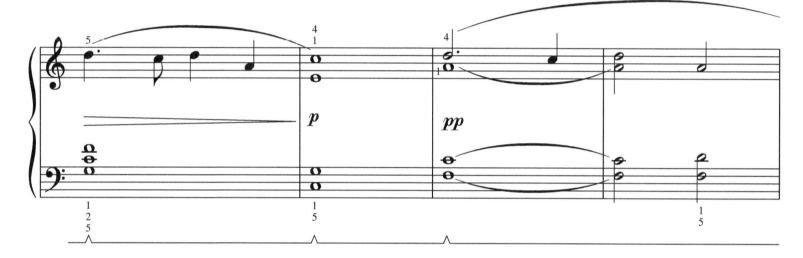

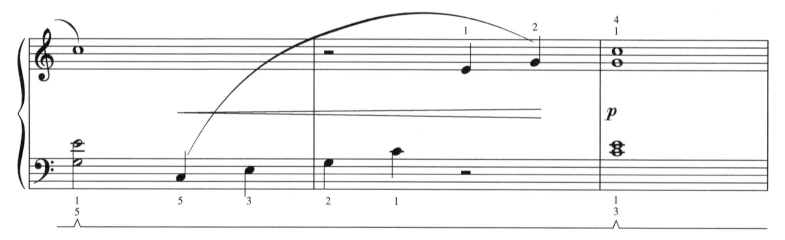

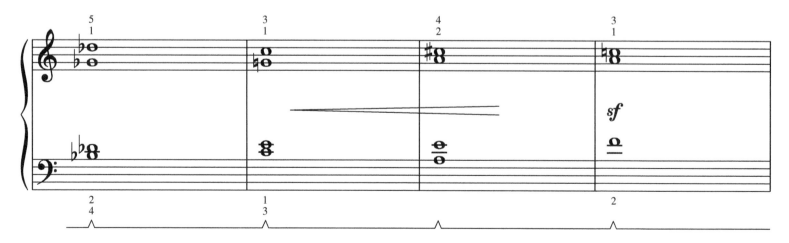

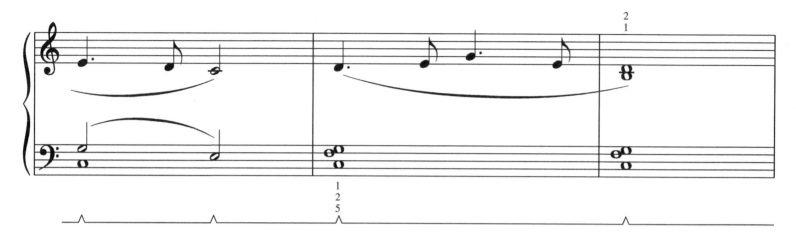

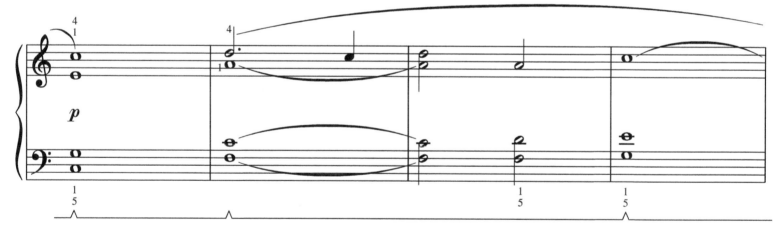

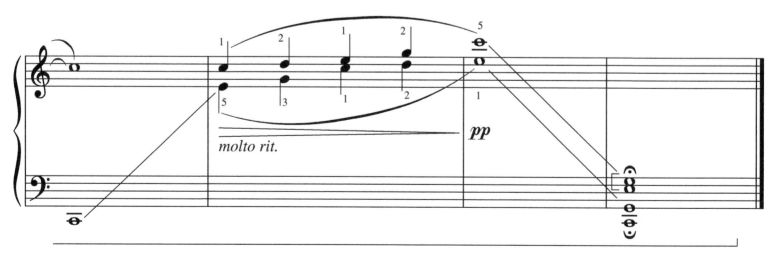

HALLELUJAH!
from *Messiah*

George Frideric Handel
arranged by Phillip Keveren

Allegro

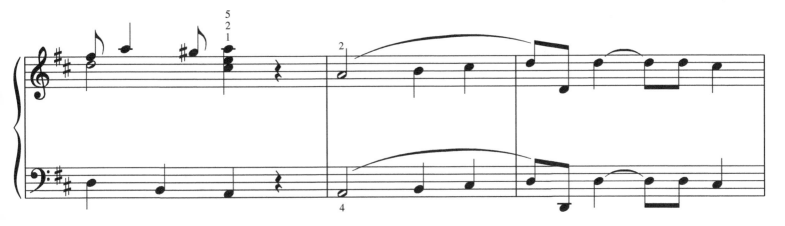

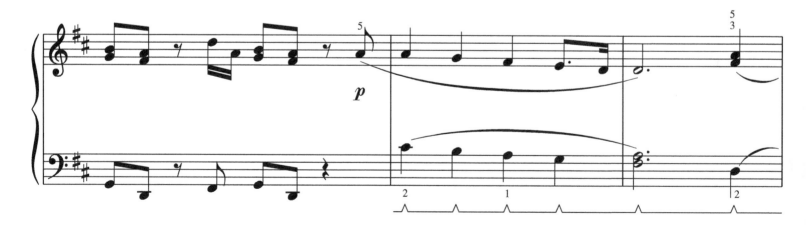

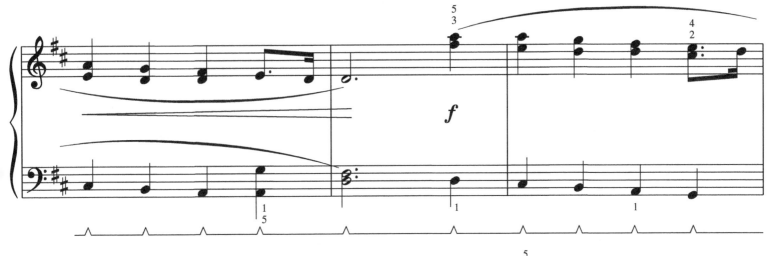

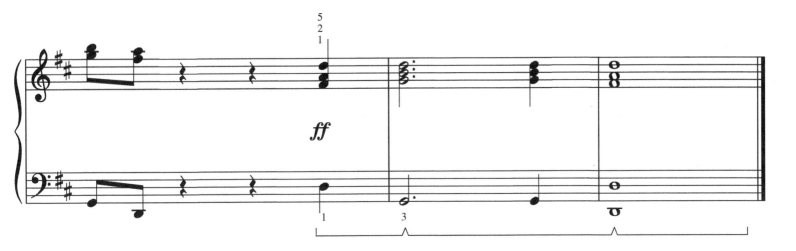

SICILIENNE

Gabriel Fauré
arranged by Phillip Keveren

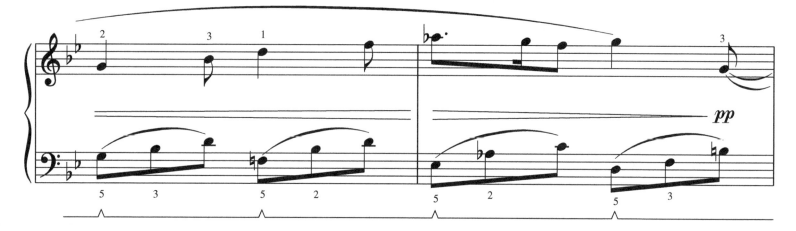

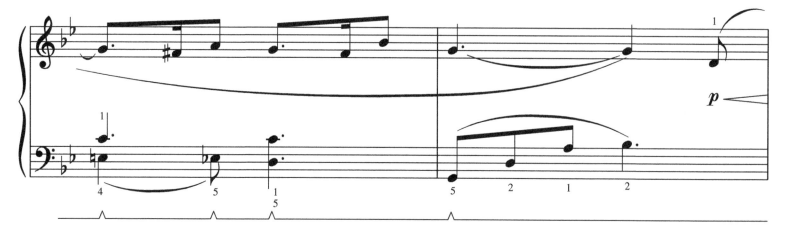

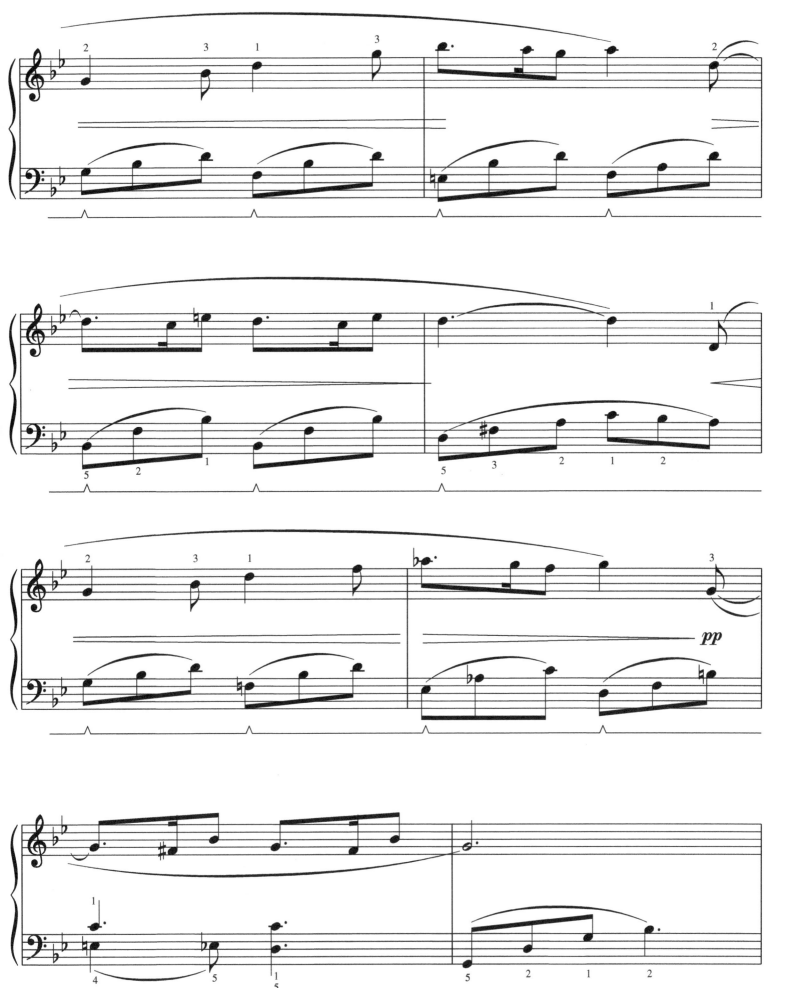

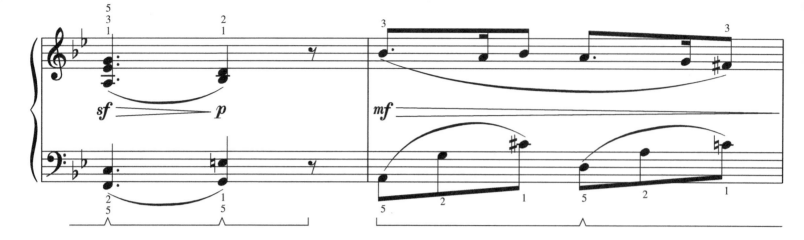

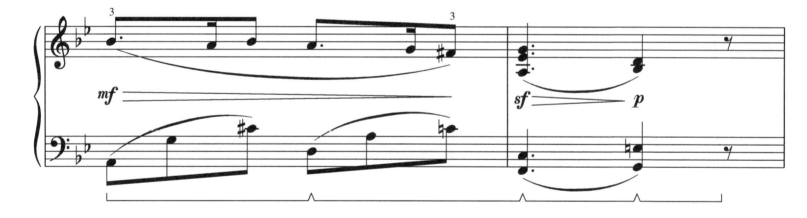

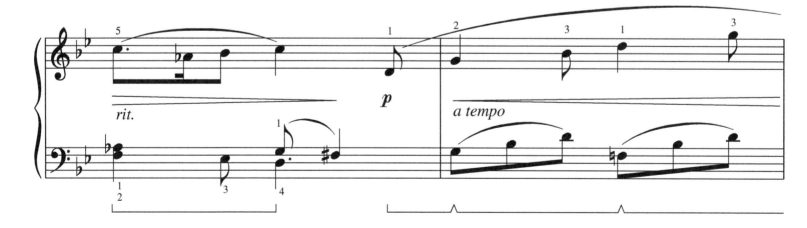

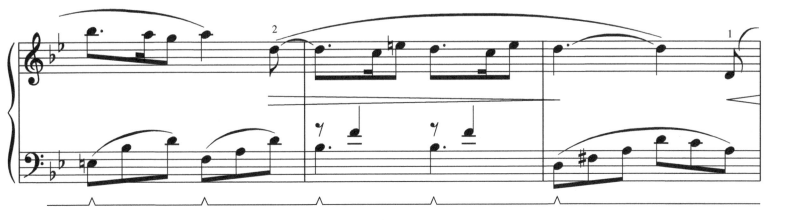

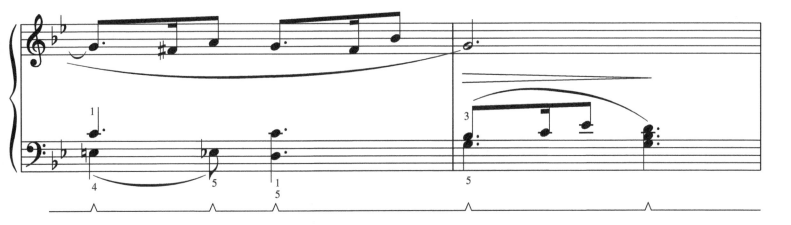

AVE MARIA

Charles Gounod
based on "Prelude in C" by J.S. Bach
arranged by Phillip Keveren

Andante con moto

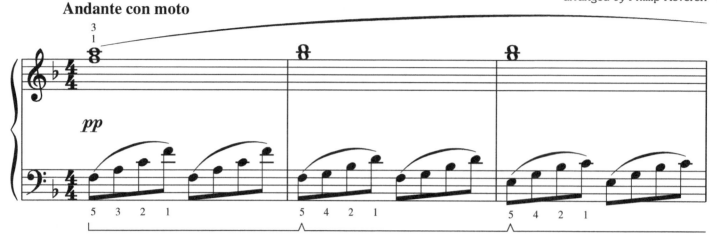

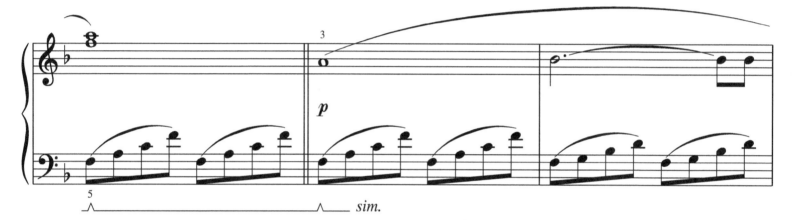

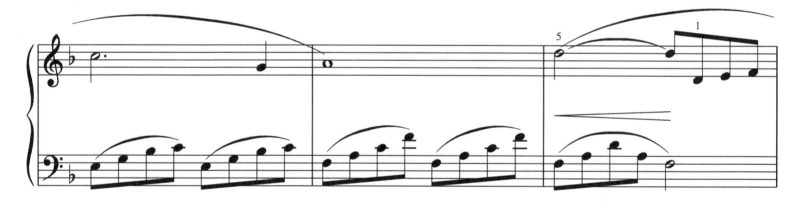

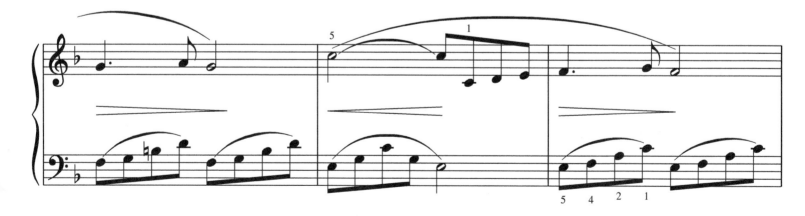

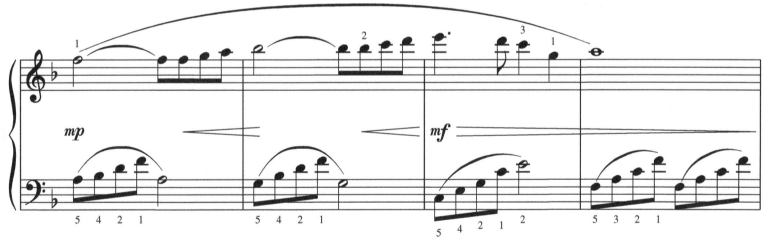

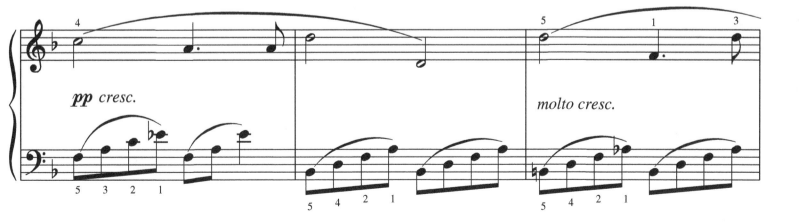

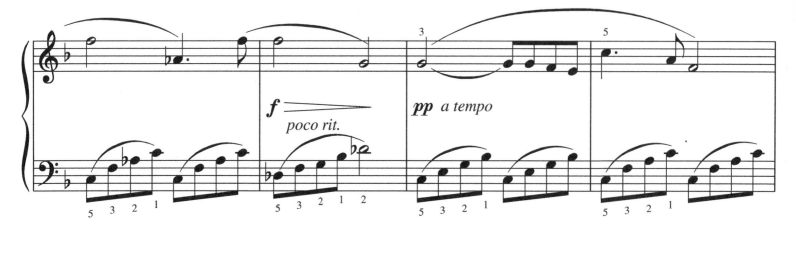

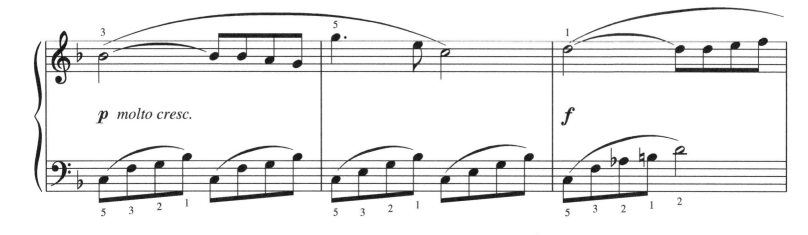

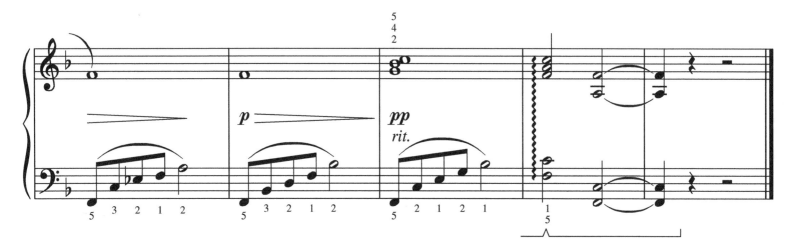

FUNERAL MARCH OF A MARIONETTE

Charles Gounod
arranged by Phillip Keveren

Allegretto

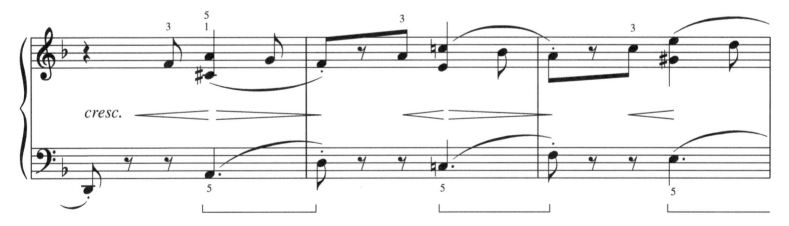

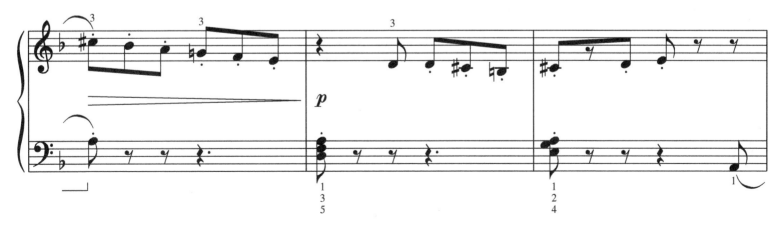

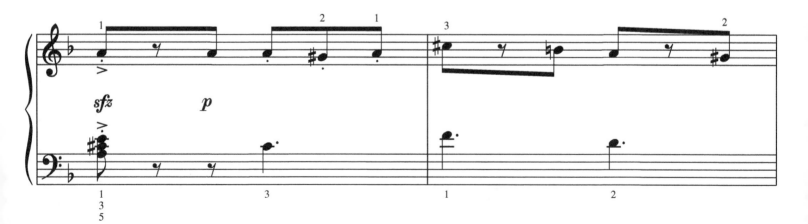

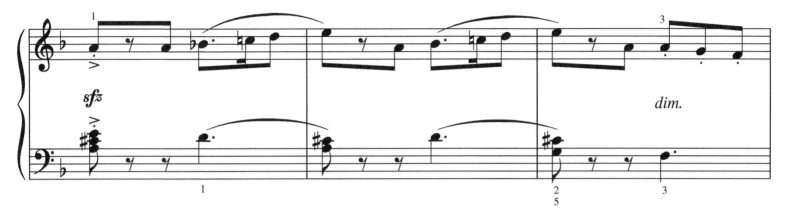

IN THE HALL OF THE MOUNTAIN KING

from *Peer Gynt*

Edvard Grieg
arranged by Phillip Keveren

March

Both hands one octave lower

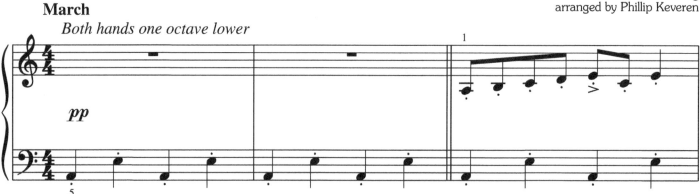

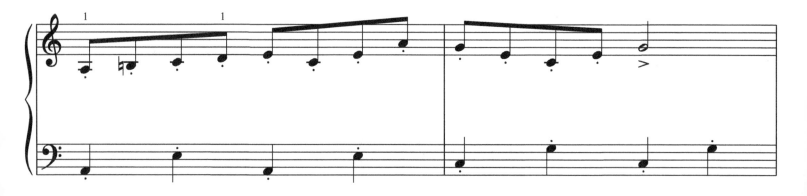

poco a poco cresc. e accel.

Both hands loco

mf

8vb

8vb

ff *vigorously*

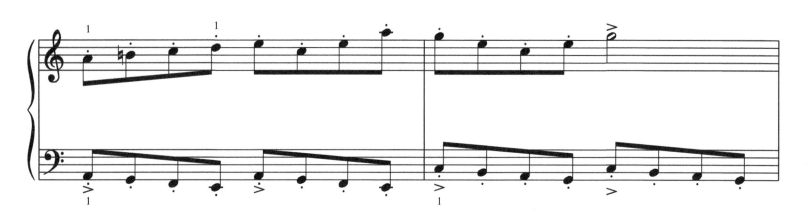

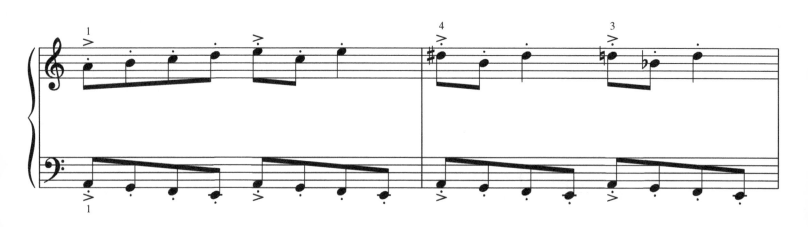

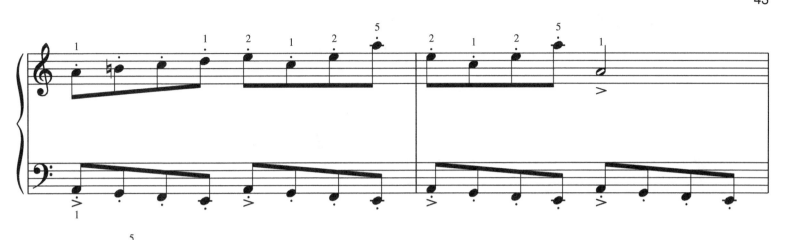

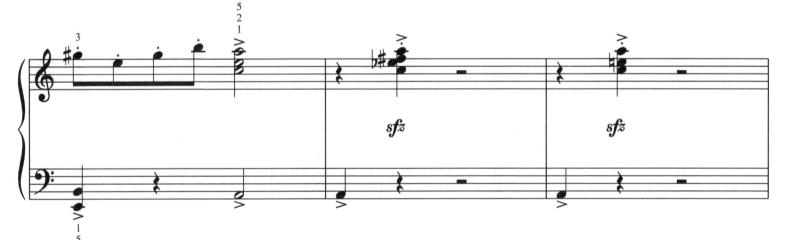

EINE KLEINE NACHTMUSIK
First Movement Excerpt

Wolfgang Amadeus Mozart
arranged by Phillip Keveren

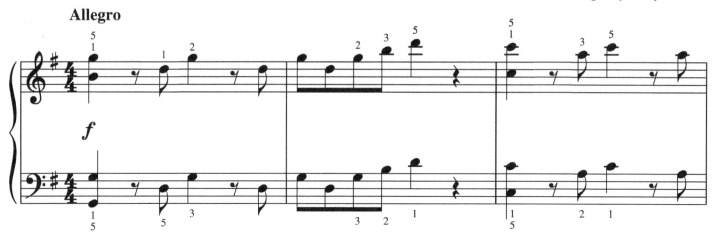

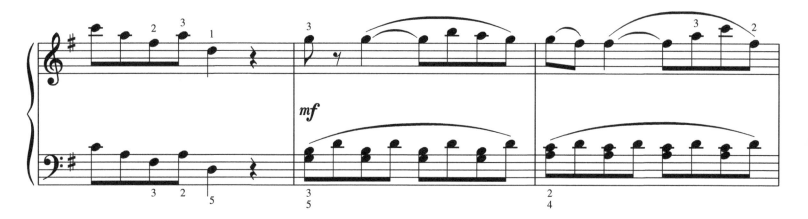

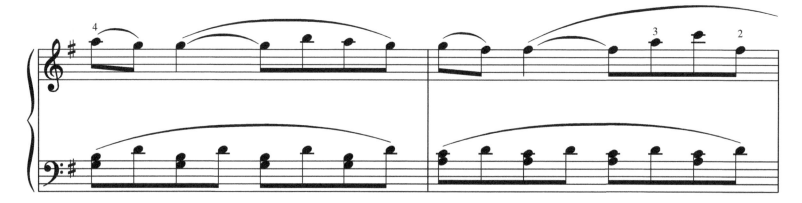

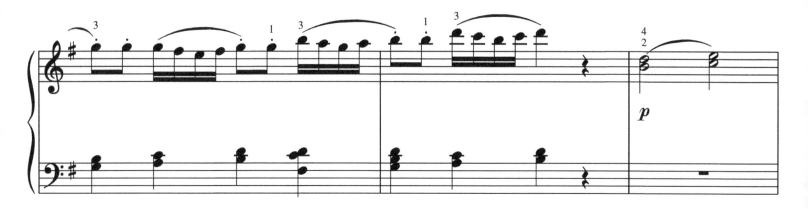

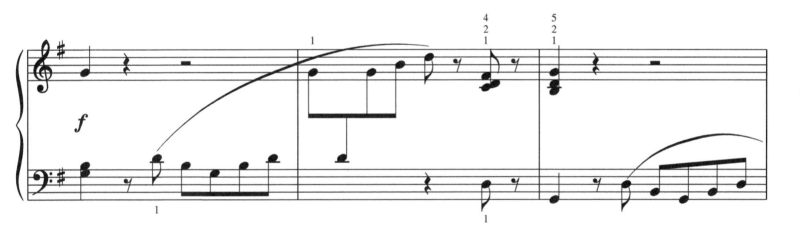

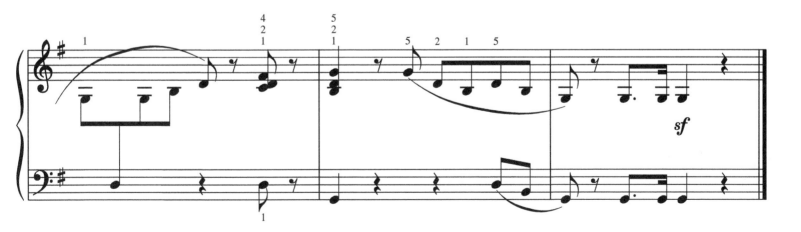

SYMPHONY NO. 40 IN G MINOR

First Movement Excerpt

Wolfgang Amadeus Mozart
arranged by Phillip Keveren

Allegro molto

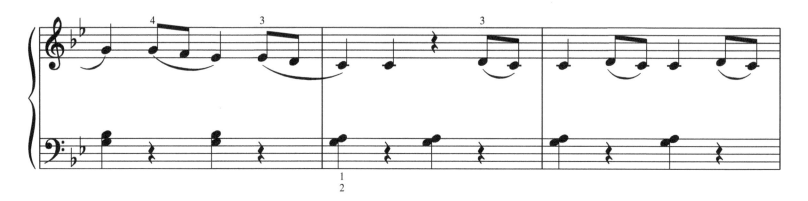

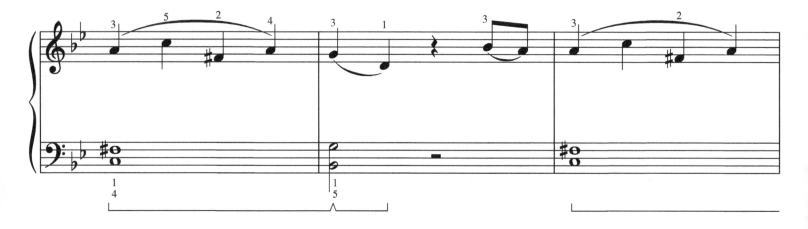

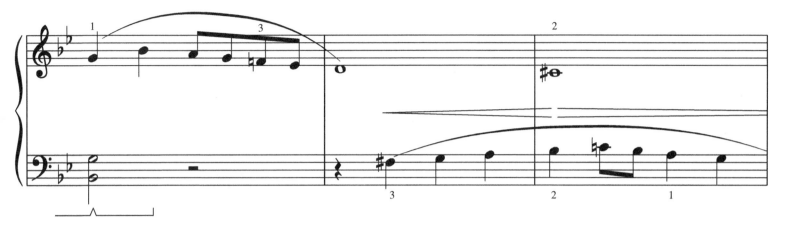

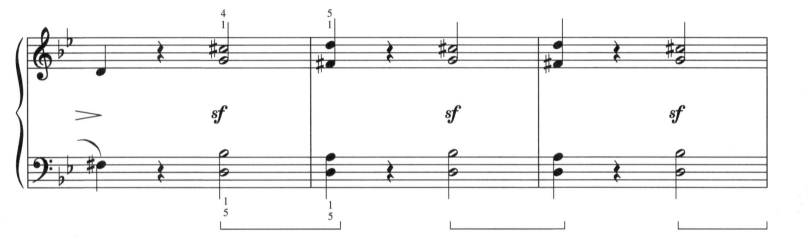

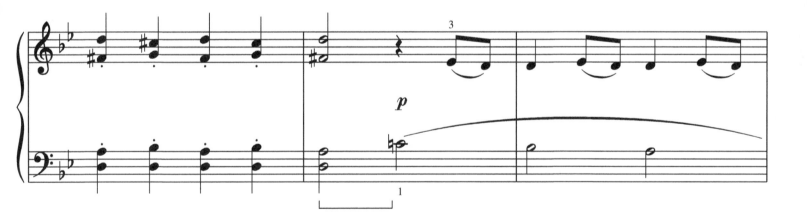

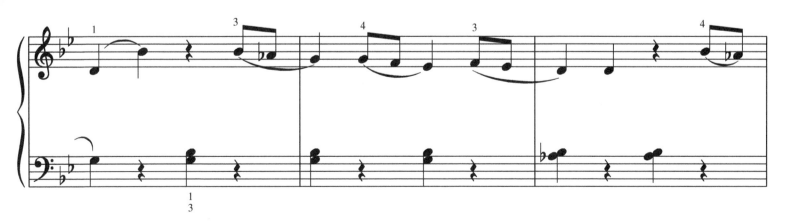

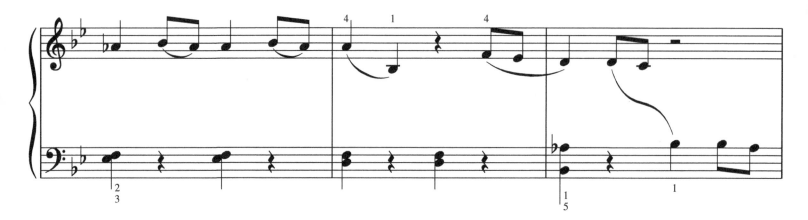

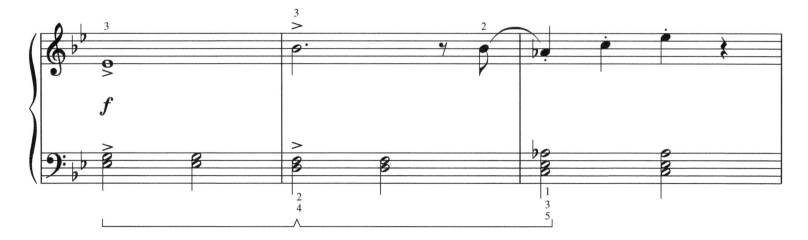

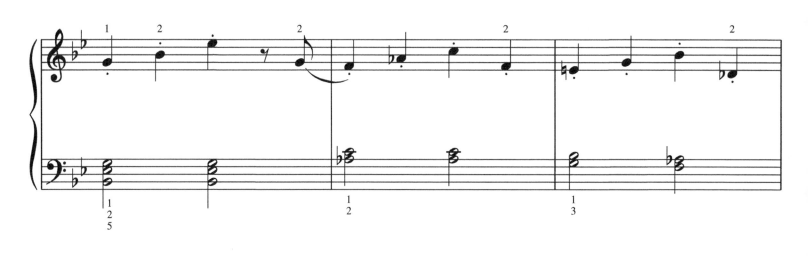

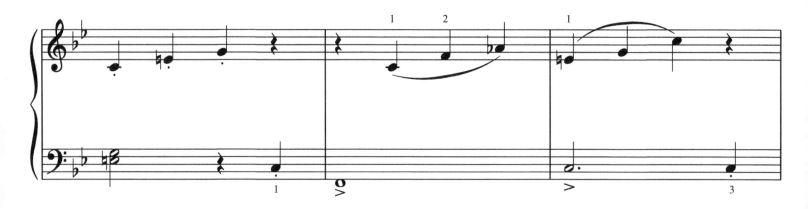

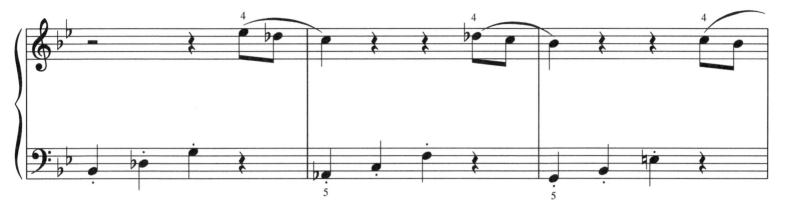

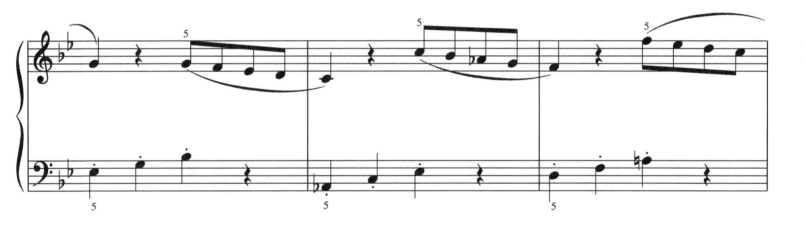

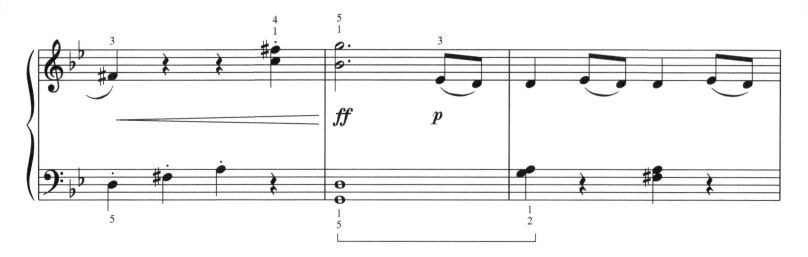

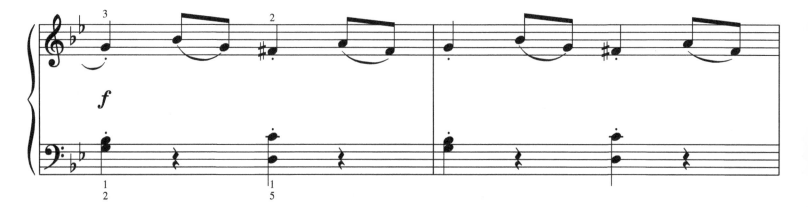

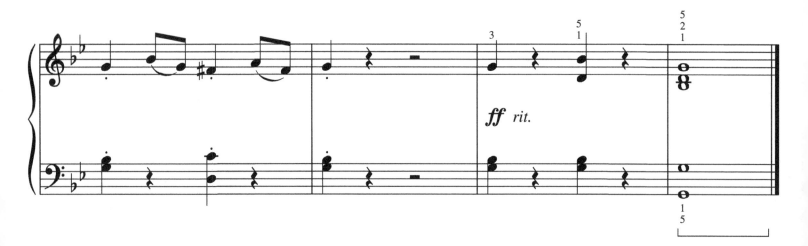

CAN CAN

from *Orpheus in the Underworld*

Jacques Offenbach
arranged by Phillip Keveren

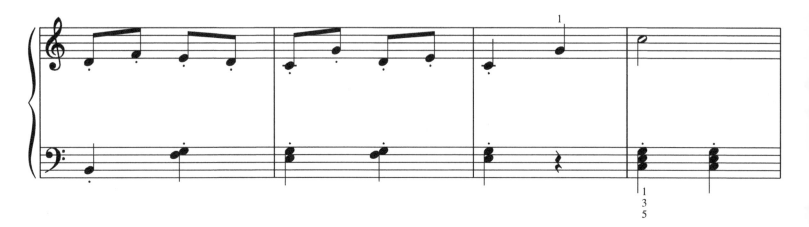

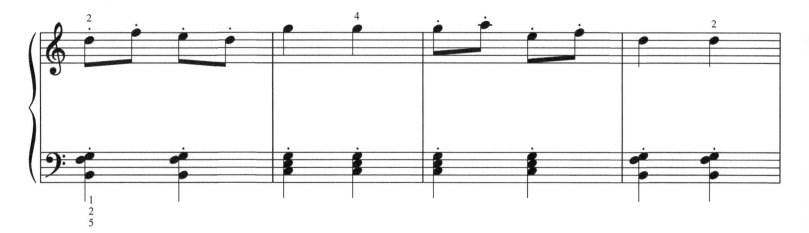

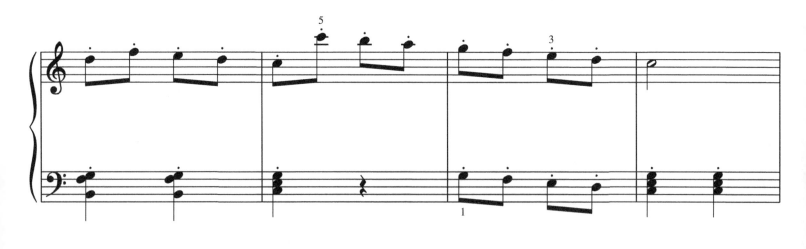

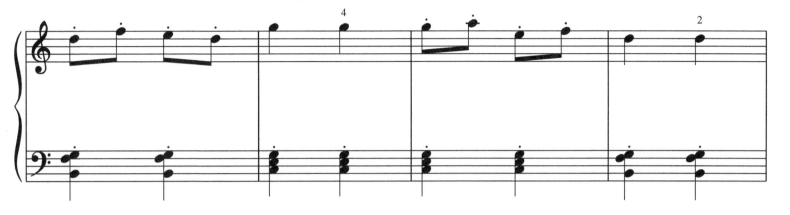

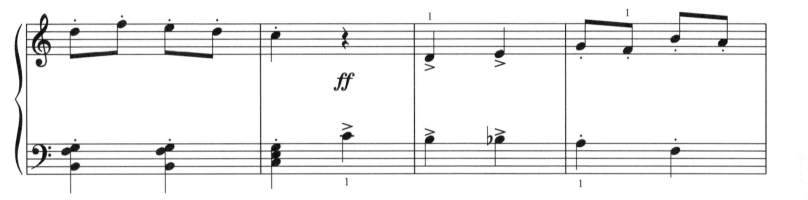

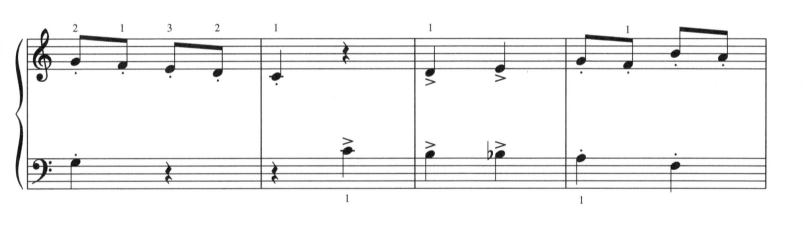

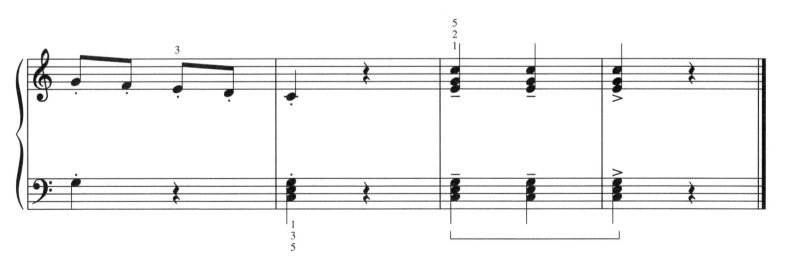

CANON IN D MAJOR

Johann Pachelbel
arranged by Phillip Keveren

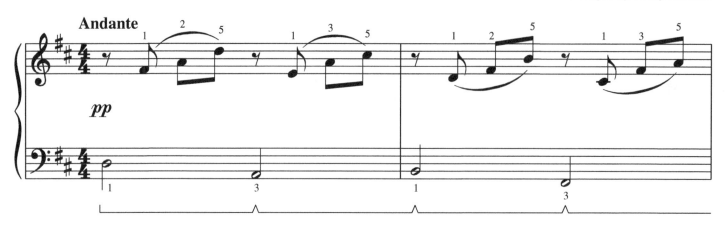

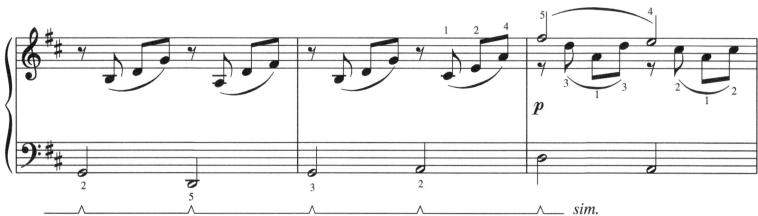

cresc. poco a poco

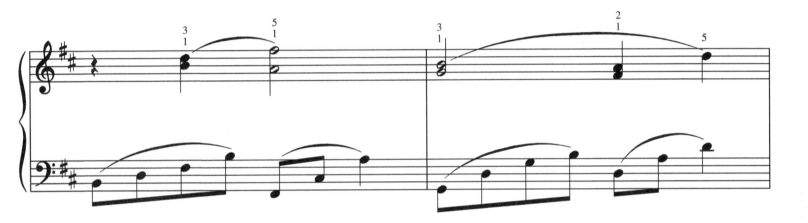

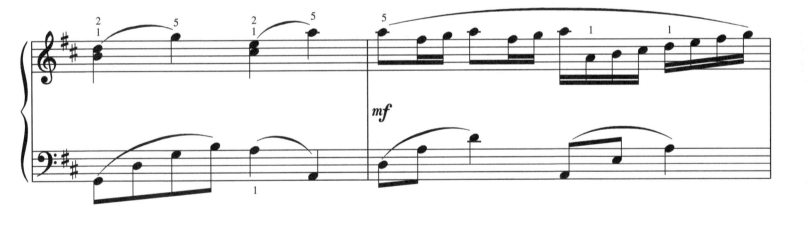

mf

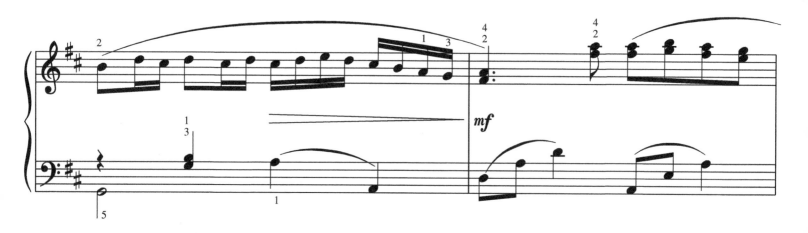

EMPEROR WALTZ

Johann Strauss, Jr.
arranged by Phillip Keveren

Tempo di Valse

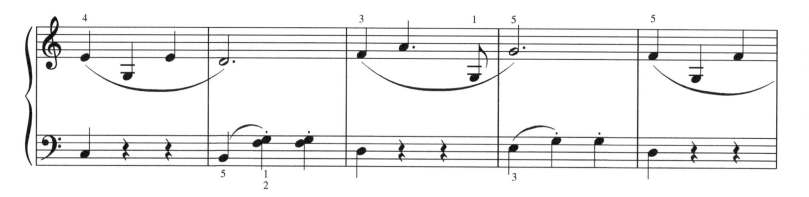

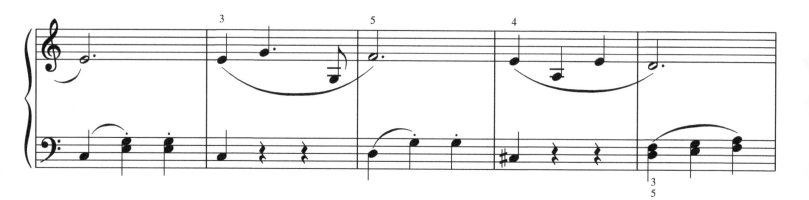

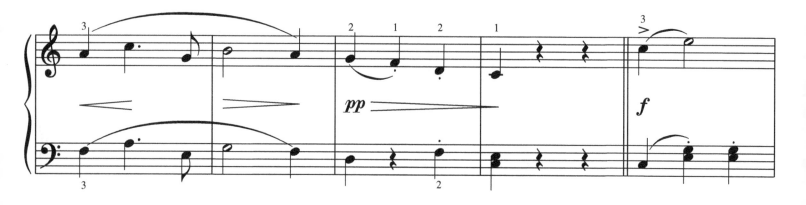

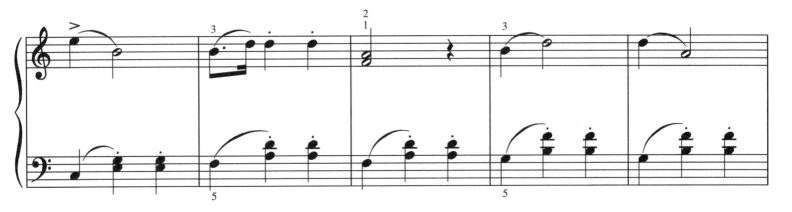

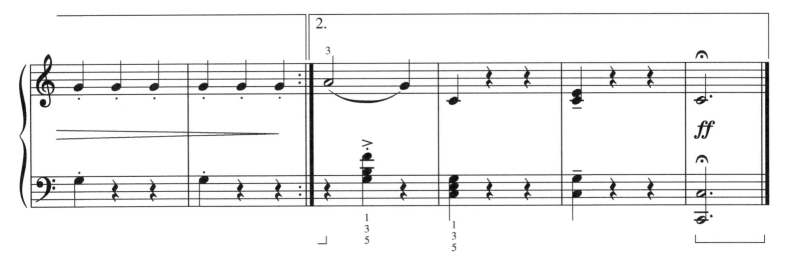

LA DONNA È MOBILE
from *Rigoletto*

Giuseppe Verdi
arranged by Phillip Keveren

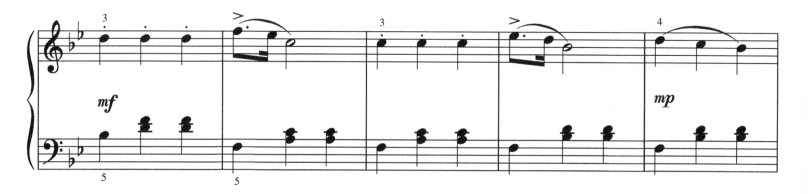

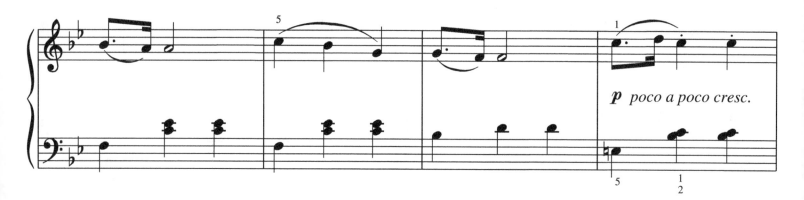

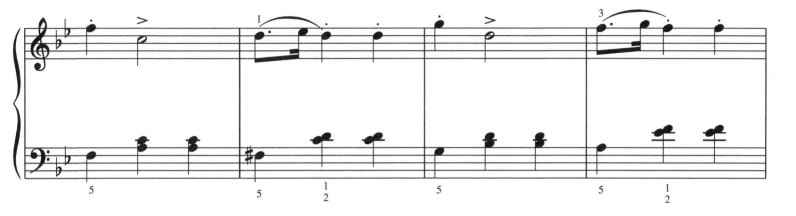

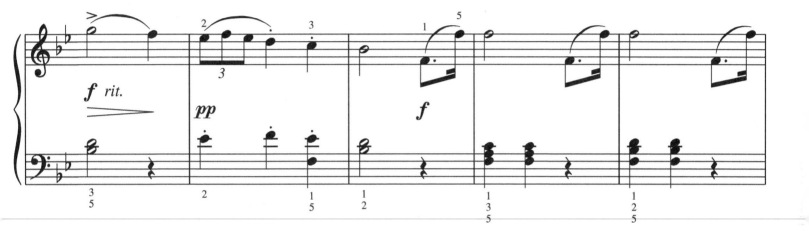

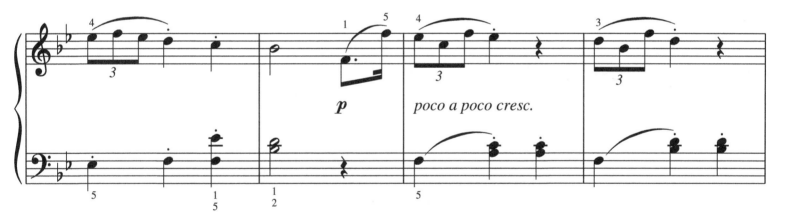

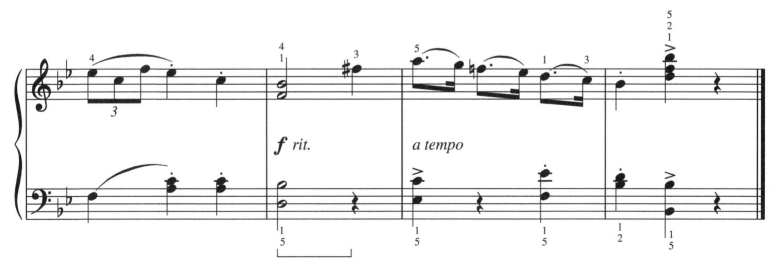

ROMEO AND JULIET
"Love Theme"

Pyotr Il'yich Tchaikovsky
arranged by Phillip Keveren

Andante con moto

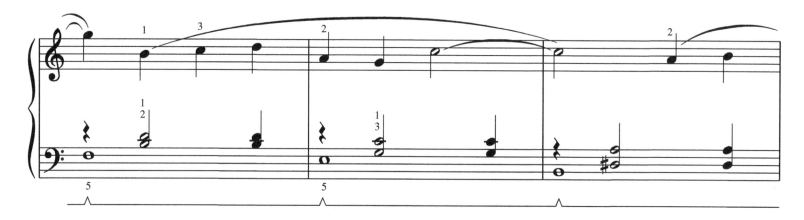

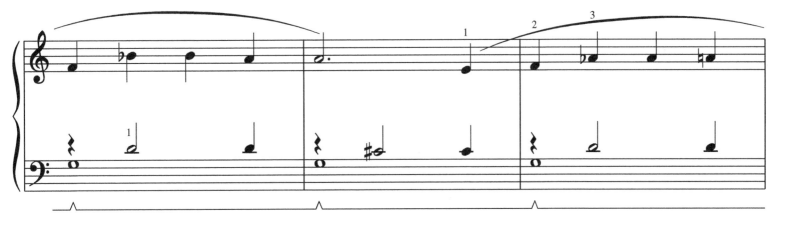

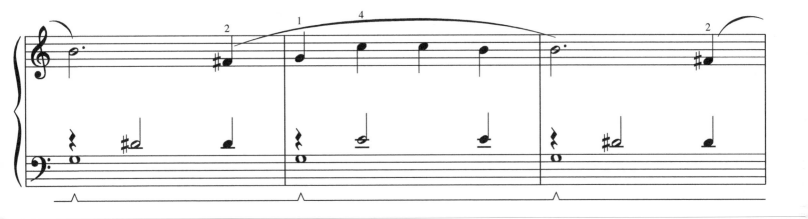

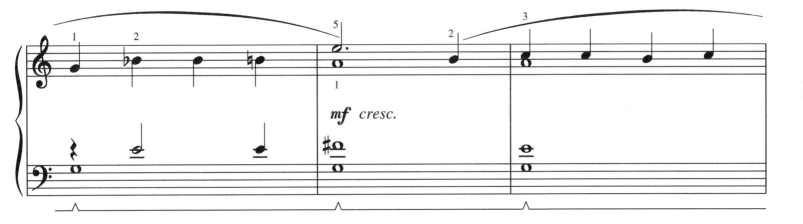

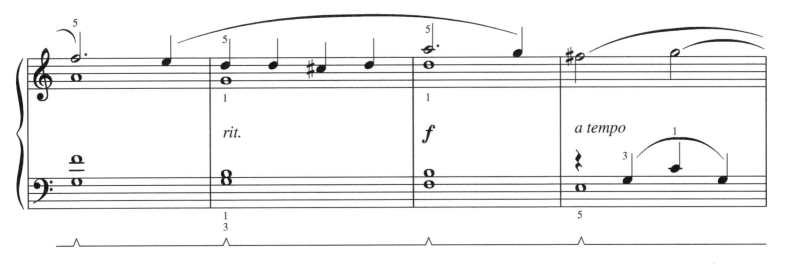

64

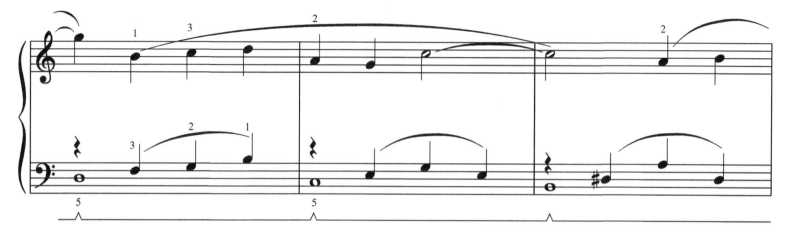

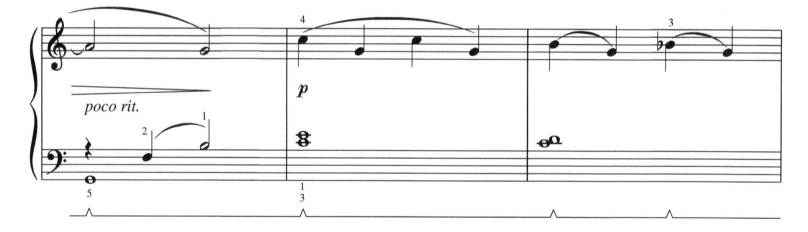

SWAN LAKE
Principal Theme

Pyotr Il'yich Tchaikovsky
arranged by Phillip Keveren

66

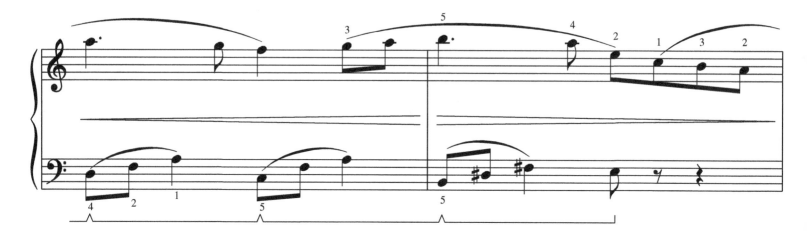

Slightly faster

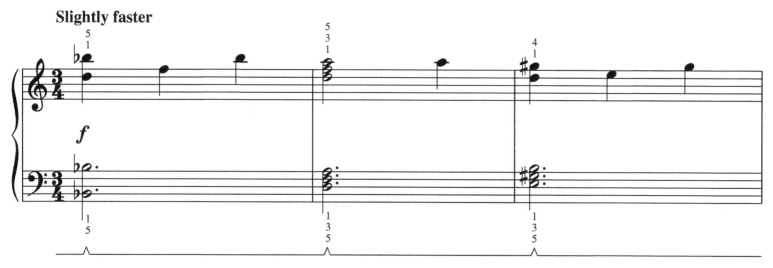

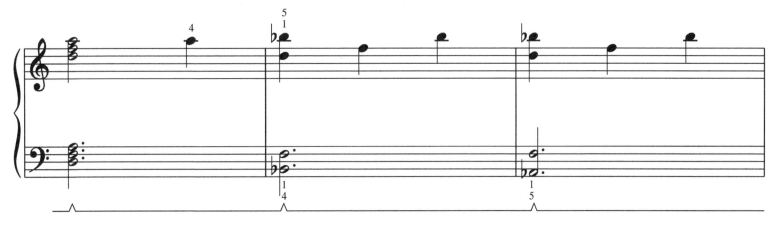

Maestoso

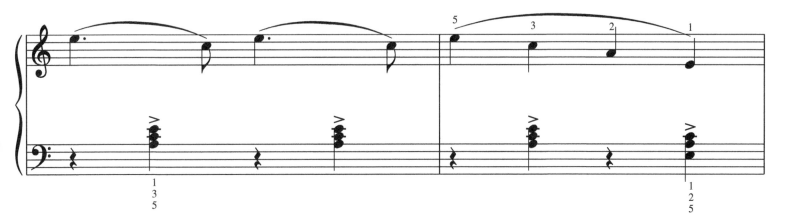

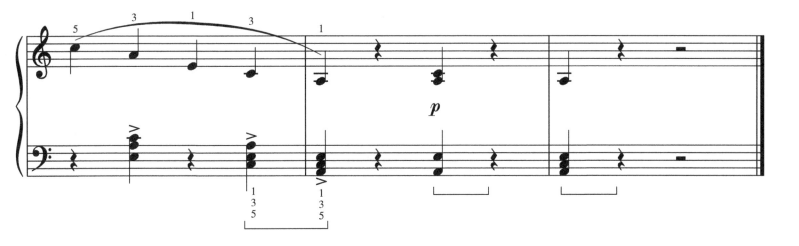

WALTZ OF THE FLOWERS

from *The Nutcracker*

Pyotr Il'yich Tchaikovsky
arranged by Phillip Keveren

Tempo di Valse

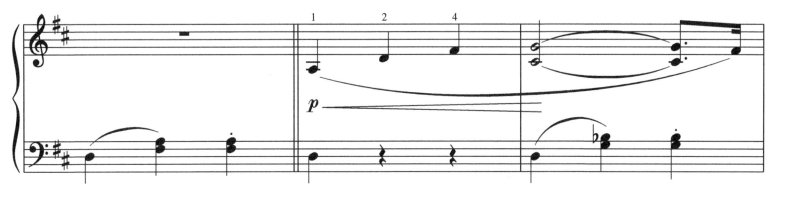

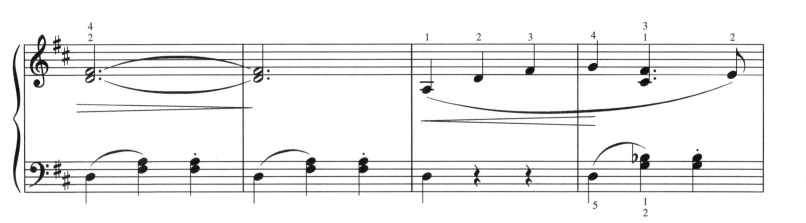

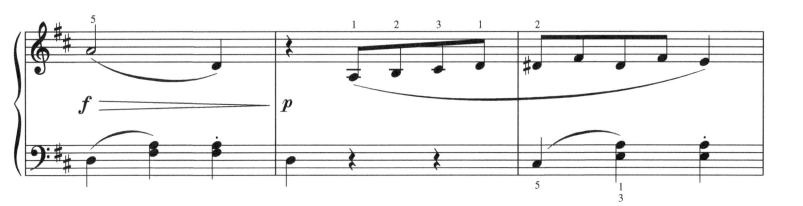

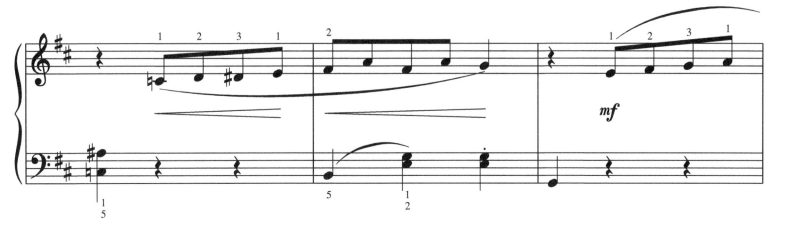

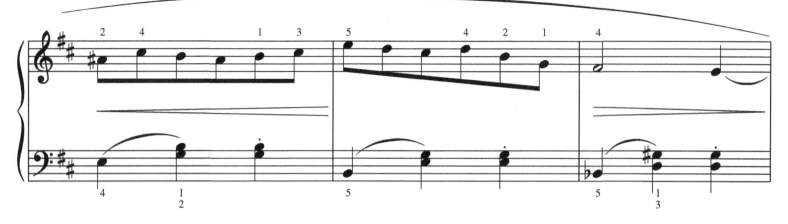

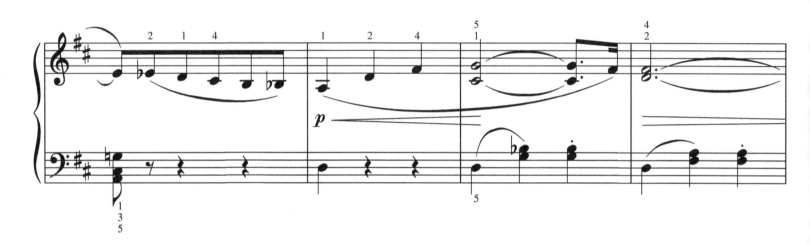

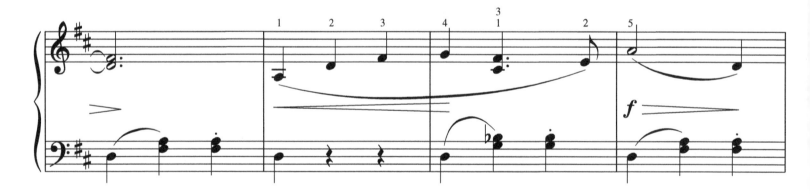

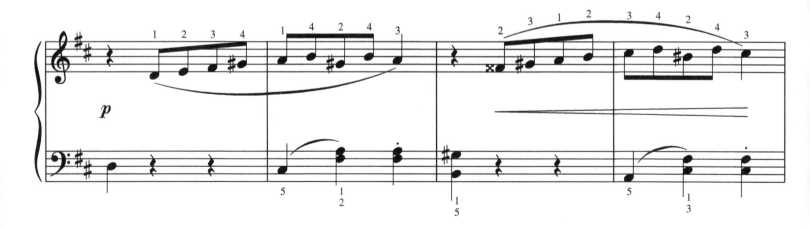

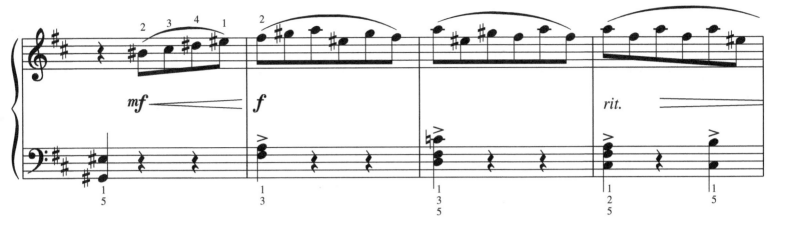

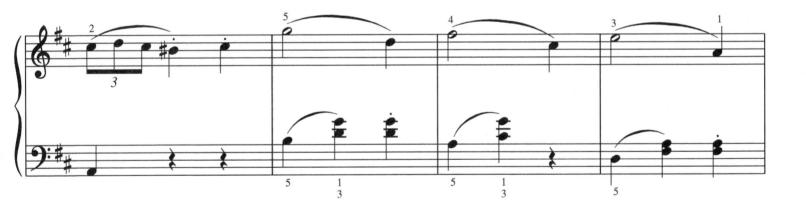

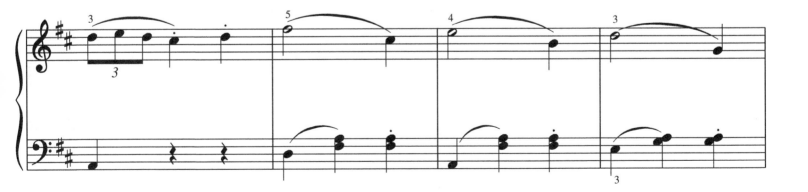

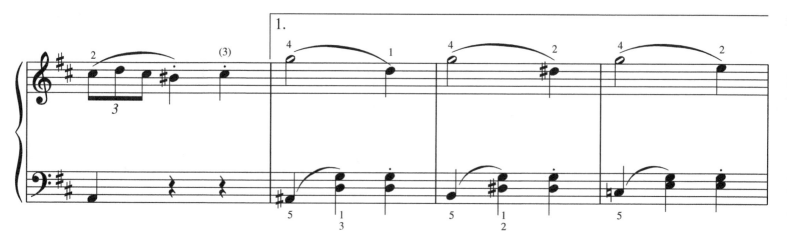

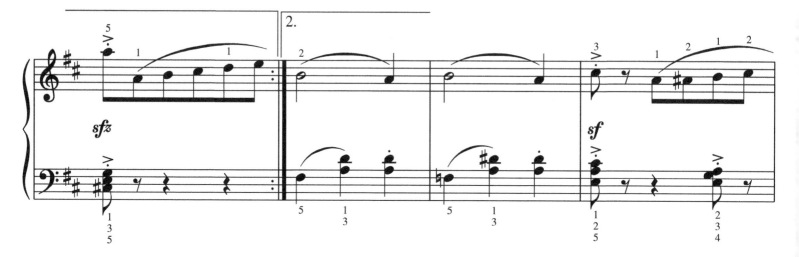